Little Chanakya

Fight Corona@School

-Essential children's guide for do's and don't for back to school-

₹75

Little Chanakya And Back TO School

Story - Rinkal sharma   Illustration and Inking - Prabhat srivastava

SS PUBLIC SCHOOL
Welcome Back to School!
Thank you ma'am!
Ma'am, this machine is not working, what to do now?
Show me, uncle.
Really, it's working now.
Very good, Arjun.
Arjun is Technology Expert

Assembly Time
Children, currently the whole world is fighting against the Corona pandemic. To protect ourselves and our loved ones, we all have to follow its rules. That's why, we should keep a proper distance from each other, wear masks and follow all the rules written on the school notice boards.
Bali, sit on the next seat.
Why?
We cannot sit together during Covid time.
Classroom
See! Only one child will sit on one seat and no one will share their lunch, pen, pencil or notebook with other. Bali, you are the distance monitor, now.
Ok ma'am.

Radha, wear your mask properly.
Sorry ma'am, I forgot.
Now onwards you will never forget. You are the mask monitor of the class and it is your responsibility to see that every child wears the mask.
Dhananjay, put on your mask.
I have trouble in breathing. Huhh! What if my immunity and lungs become weak....
Please calm down Bali.
I won't spare Dhananjay....
I have brought laddoos for you, Bali.
Bali's anger is pacified after hearing of laddoos
What will happen with these circles and this social distancing?
Hihihih!! They might help us while playing the game 'Langadi'.

Lunch time
Hihihih!! Tinku, your mask is wet now.
Don't put on the wet mask as it increases the chance of Infection rather than controlling Corona virus.
Washroom
After lunch, Pihu goes to the washroom. she sanitizes her hands after coming out of the washroom.

Friends, please do maintain some distance.
Uff! This Corona has banned sitting, playing, eating with my friends.
I am feeling bored at school.
Chanakya, do something as everyone is troubled by these Covid rules.
Hmm... I have to think about something
Chanakya's intellegence always work
How low is students' attendance.
Yes, there are only 10 kids in my class.
NOTICE
1. Keep Distance
2. Wear mask
Only 12 in my class.

Chanakya goes to his class teacher
Indeed Chanakya! It's a great idea.
SCHOOL NOTICE BOARD
1. TWO PEOPLE SHOULD NOT WALK TOGETHER ON THE STAIRS.
2. KEEP PROPER DISTANCE WITH OTHER.
3. DO NOT TOUCH THE RAILING OF THE STAIRS.
4. ALWAYS WEAR YOUR MASK.

After lunch, free period is going on in the class
Shewwww!!

Friends, don't touch each other's things like this.
(Angrily) why?
Let me explain. Radha, Bali and Tina come here.
Suppose, Bali is a Corona patient and this chalk powder is Corona Virus. Now, Bali, blow this powder hard.
Bali removes the mask and blow the chalk powder.
Look friends! Similarly, while speaking, sneezing or coughing, the corona virus can also spread from person to person through droplets or by the things touched by the corona patient, that is why proper distance and mask is very important.
He's right.
Radha is affected and Tina is saved, due to social distancing.
No one is as inteligent as Chanakya

Very good Chanakya! There is a mask and slogan activity on Saturday, whosoever wants to participate, tell me your name. All the children will bring their photo wearing mask and yoga mats to do yoga after assembly.
Children who go by bus will assemble at Gate number 1 and those who are accompanied by their parents should go to Gate number 2.
Children are sitting on the seats as they were placed in the morning.

Chanakya, a message has come from your school that due to corona, this time your unit tests will be conducted online and objective type.
Great!
Runjhun, you should also wear a mask.
Ohh noo!!
After the assembly all the children are doing yoga in the ground.
Today you all will have your activity class in the ground and some rewards will also be given.

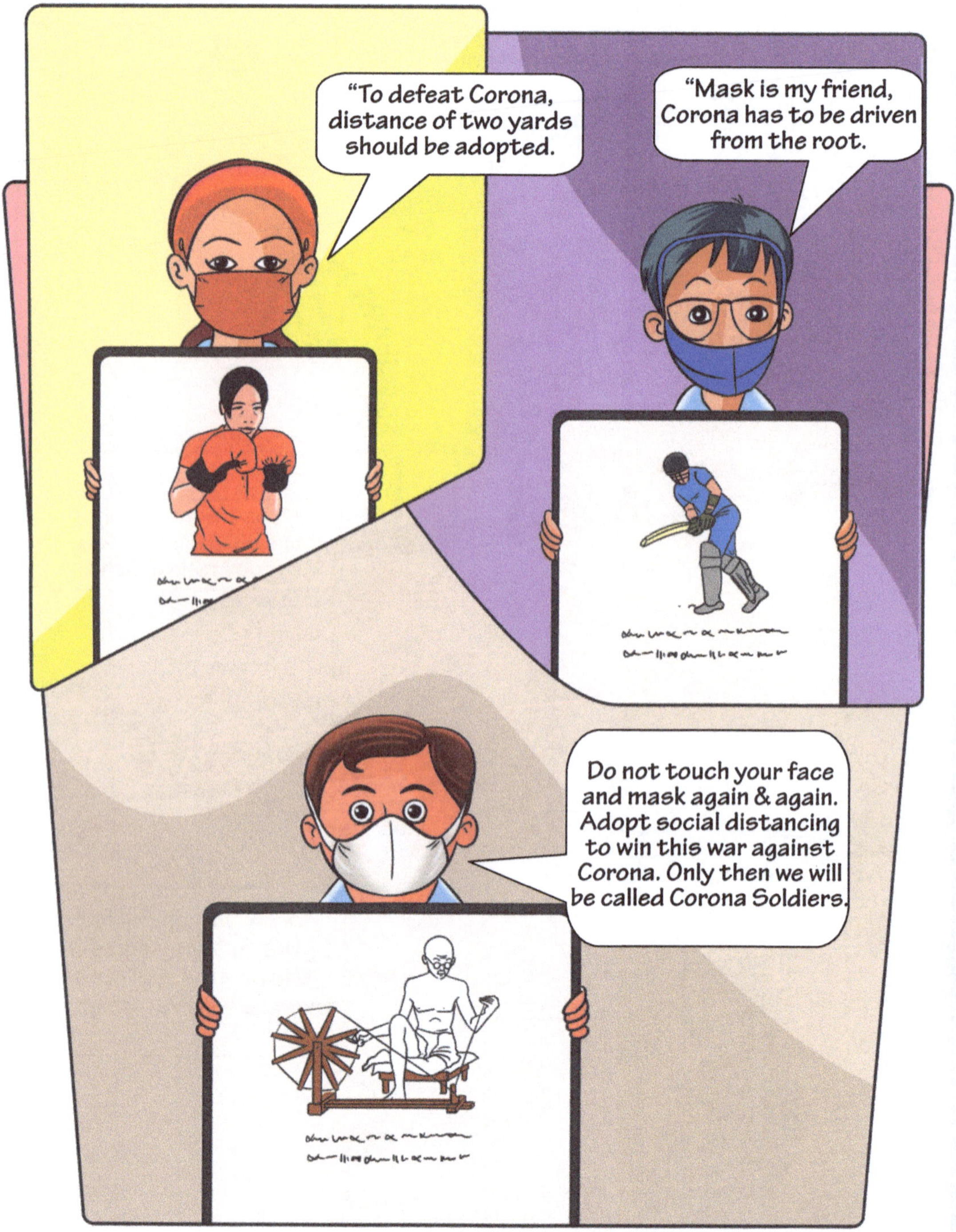
"To defeat Corona, distance of two yards should be adopted.
"Mask is my friend, Corona has to be driven from the root.
Do not touch your face and mask again & again. Adopt social distancing to win this war against Corona. Only then we will be called Corona Soldiers.

Wearing mask and a distance of two yards is our only slogan of the present, to make India Corona free is our only religion.
If you feel restless while eating or running, then it is necessary to avoid the mask but beware of the crowd thus wear your mask and maintain the distance.
Chanakya tells the right way to wear mask
Not on your ears
Not below your nose

Not on your chin.
Not on your head.
Cover your nose and mouth properly, This is the right way.
'Mask star of the week' goes to Dhananjay and 'The best distance star of the week' goes to Arjun.

Thank you Radha, and sorry for that day.
It's ok.
Chanakya, indeed your idea was very good. Now, once again all the students are going to their school.
'Best student of the week' goes to Chanakya
Thank you ma'am
Pictures of all the winners with their masks are put on the board.
NOTICE BOARD
Don't remove mask
Follow social distancing

Little Chanakya And Handwash

Story - Rinkal sharma   Illustration and Inking - Prabhat srivastava

Bali angrily lifts Dhananjay up in the air.
It was by chance.
Why did you sneeze intentionally?
Dhishoom!
Now have a punch 'by chance'.
Hearing about laddoos, Bali calms down.
Bali, leave Dhananjay aside. I have brought laddoos for you in the lunch.
See, I dropped him.
Ahh!! [painfully]
Chanakya, why did you let him go?
Don't worry! Will teach him a lesson later.

Children, in this Friday assembly it is the turn of our section for carol sing-ing. Our theme is- Hand hygiene. Chanakya, you are the activity leader.
Ok ma'am.
Ma'am, how does a virus or a micro germ spread?
Ma'am, can I tell?
Chanakya hand is filled with blue ink and then he shakes with Pihu
Hello Pihu!
(smiling) Hihi-hihi Hello!
(smiling) In the same way any virus or micro organism gets transferred to one another.
Chhii!! My hand.

Wash your hands thoroughly with this liquid soap before preparing the food (sudama).
Mom, shall I go for a bicycle ride?
Sure, but do wash your hands once you return.
Chanakya, we have to do something of Dhananjay.
We have to teach him a lesson.
Don't worry friends! Let me think.
All children gather in the corridor with their bicycles.
Radha, would you like to have chocolate?
Just a minute. Let me sanitize my hands first.
Radha can understand animal's language
Bhow..Bhow.. (Radha, sanitize my hands too)
Yaaahooo...hoooooooo...yeeeeii
Let me help you Chanakya.

Pihu has some blur sense.
(mumbling) Hmm!! Gimmick
(speaks) Have you seen something….a boy…..problem
WASHROOM
Dhananjay hears some noise from the washroom. Hahaha our prey has come…will not leave it now…time to make him sick..hahahaha.
(fearing) Wh…wh… who is there?
10 STEPS
Gasping…. fffffffsssssss
During lunch Dhananjay goes to the school washroom.
Dhananjay returns to his class in fear. Sweat starts pouring from his forehead and his breath becomes even faster.

What happened? Why are you so scared?
Share with us. We will help you.
There must be a ghost.
Let's go and see.
Oh my God! Corona virus...
Arjuna eyes are scanners.
Oh no! Then it must be on Dhananjay's hands too.... You are about to be sick.
Run! Run!
All the children run away in fear.

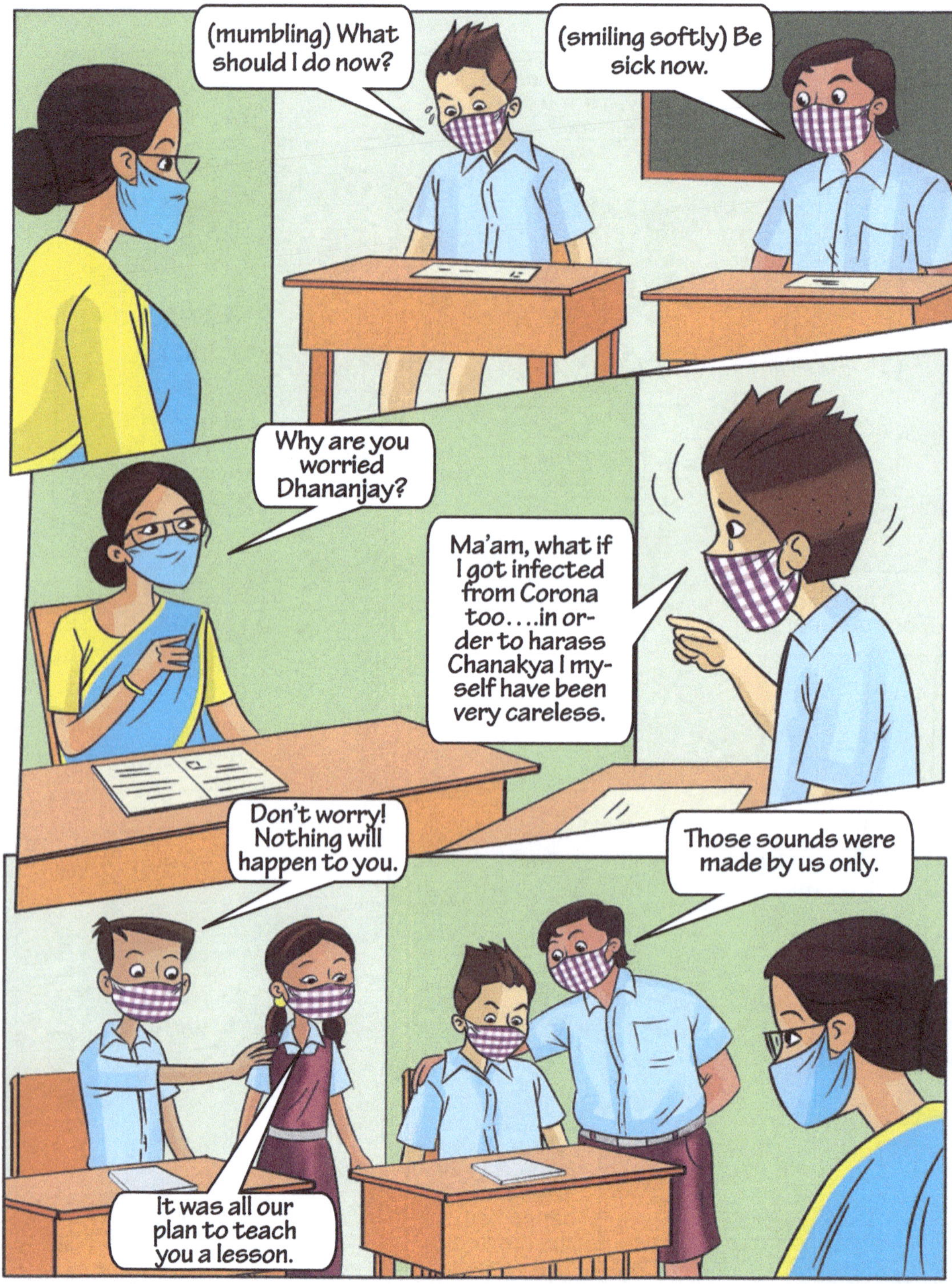
(mumbling) What should I do now?
(smiling softly) Be sick now.
Why are you worried Dhananjay?
Ma'am, what if I got infected from Corona too....in order to harass Chanakya I myself have been very careless.
Don't worry! Nothing will happen to you.
It was all our plan to teach you a lesson.
Those sounds were made by us only.

Dhananjay, don't be afraid! There is no corona virus in the school. If you wash your hands thoroughly with soap or use sanitizer after sneezing, coughing, playing, touching anything or any pets before and after eating and drinking, then you have no fear of infection. You should take care of your safety and that of your companions too.
Chanakya told me everything. Always keep one thing in mind that the one who thinks bad of others, does bad to his own.
(Lowering his head in shame) Yes ma'am.
Have you understood or should we explain?
It's ok dear.
(holding his ears) Sorry Chanakya. Will not do this mistake again.

Oh no!
This was a real one friends.
Chanakya! Your idea was superb.
Now Dhananjay will never tease us.
He has now changed.
Chanakya and all his companions are sitting in the society park.
Sorry Gabbar.
A dog's tail will never be straight
Bow! Bow!

Now presenting- a carol on 'HAND HYGIENE'
In the assembly all the children, teachers and the principal are gathered and standing in circles with their masks on.
Chanakya, Radha, Dhananjay, Arjuna, Bali, Pihu and many other students begin to at the stage.
Let us make life healthy by
adopting hand hygiene,
Cook and eat food with
washed hands,
Either play, go to washroom or
pampering the animals,
Rub and shine your hands
with clean water and soap,
Wash your hands with clean
towel and let them smell good,
Do not shake your hands with
strangers and your loved ones,
Do not touch your nose, eyes
and face again and again,
Wear clean mask with clean
hands and maintain
social distance,
Make hygiene your weapon
to fight against diseases.

Little Chanakya And vaccination unlimited

Story - Rinkal sharma
Illustration and Inking - Prabhat srivastava

The helpers that come to our home should also get vaccinated.
When all the children gathered in the park to play
Dhishoom!
Idea! Come friends, let's go to Fine Uncle.
Pihu has déjà vu
Friends, I saw something.
Now what?
A man is beaten up.
Oh! No.
Bhanu bhaiya, did you get vaccinated?
I got infected with Corona, so I can only get vaccinated after 6 months.
Uncle, if the helpers working in the society will not get vaccinated, then also the infection of Corona can spread. What if we children get infected..

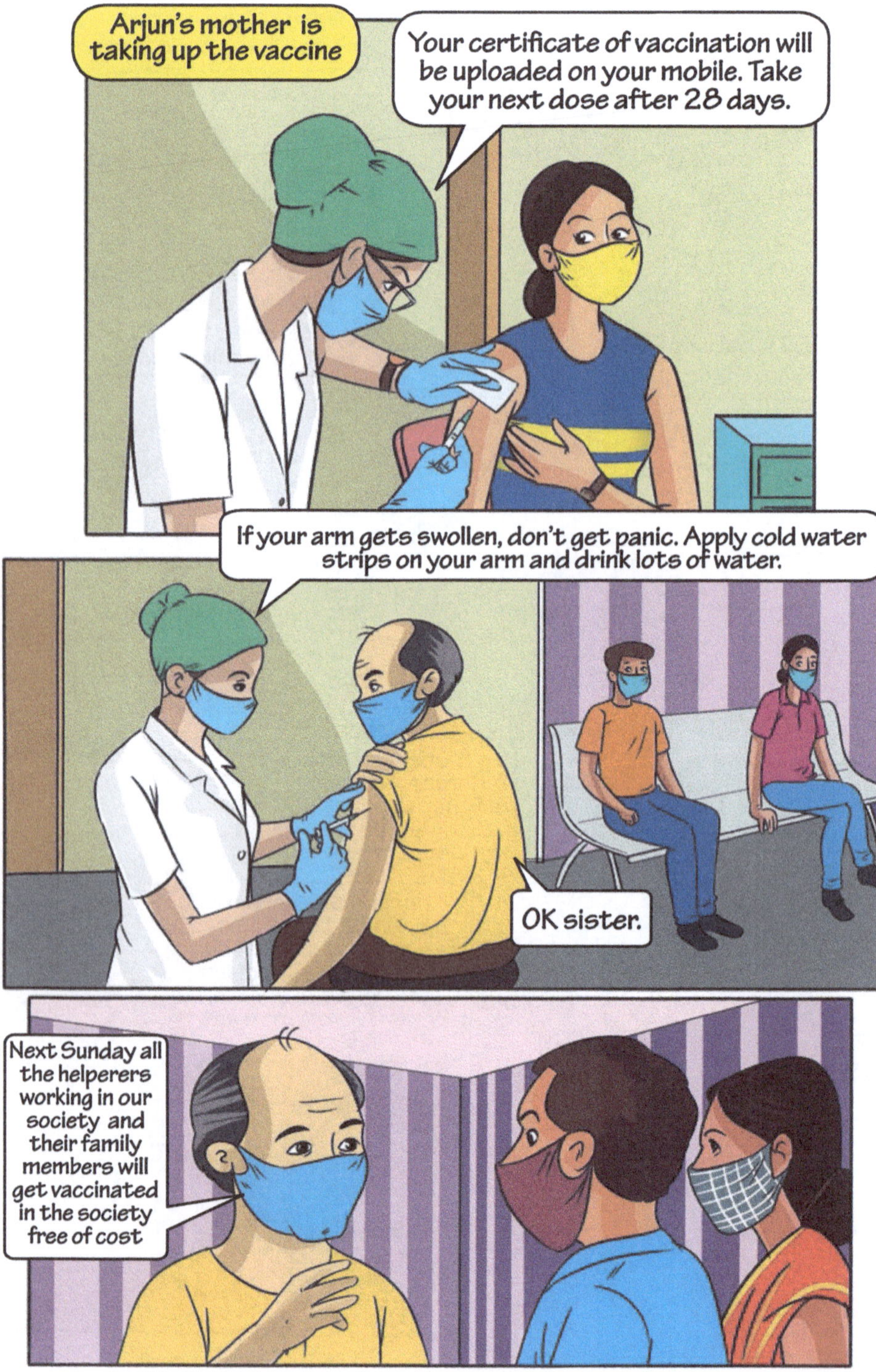
Arjun's mother is taking up the vaccine
Your certificate of vaccination will be uploaded on your mobile. Take your next dose after 28 days.
If your arm gets swollen, don't get panic. Apply cold water strips on your arm and drink lots of water.
OK sister.
Next Sunday all the helperers working in our society and their family members will get vaccinated in the society free of cost

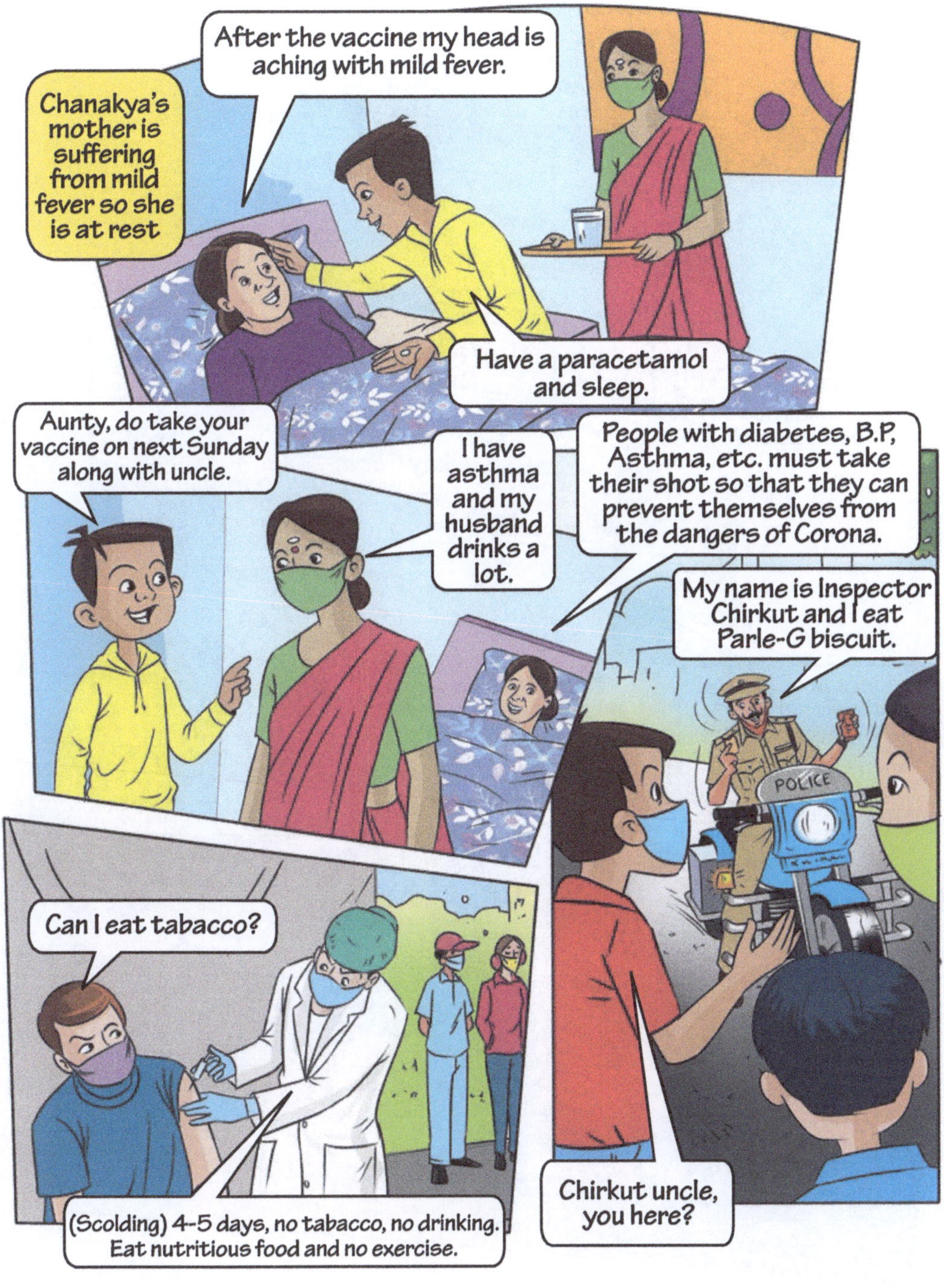
Chanakya's mother is suffering from mild fever so she is at rest
After the vaccine my head is aching with mild fever.
Have a paracetamol and sleep.
Aunty, do take your vaccine on next Sunday along with uncle.
I have asthma and my husband drinks a lot.
People with diabetes, B.P, Asthma, etc. must take their shot so that they can prevent themselves from the dangers of Corona.
My name is Inspector Chirkut and I eat Parle-G biscuit.
POLICE
Can I eat tabacco?
(Scolding) 4-5 days, no tabacco, no drinking. Eat nutritious food and no exercise.
Chirkut uncle, you here?

Inspector Chirkut asks a question
Why is it so crowded here?
Uncle, everyone is getting vaccinated here.
Did you take the permission?
Okay Good!
Here are the permission papers (while showing him the papers)
Come, let's see.
What?
Two boxes of vaccine are less.

Chirkut along with Batliwala and children, check and confirm two boxes are less.
I swear, I won't spare the thief.
I think two boxes are stolen.
First find out the thief
Chankaya intelligence always work.
Radha, quickly get Gabbar and Arjun, you also check.
Arjun eyes works like a scanner
Here are the finger prints of large fingers.
It means thief is a man
Hmmm, alcohol smell.
Alcohol smell, means thief is alcoholic.
Come, follow me
Radha understands the language of animals.

Chanakya, follow gabbar.
Chirkut uncle, follow me.
Runjhun, follow gabbar.
Okay channakya.
Chirkut tries to start his bike but as always it doesn't start and Bali helps him by pushing it forward
Thank you, Bali.
POLICE
GARRRR!! GARRRR!!!

Bali, who will be the thief?
(Angrily) Whoever it is, will get beaten up.
He is sudama's husband.
Here's the thief.
THAYE THAYE!!
Leave him.
BEAT HIM! BEAT HIM!
He steals. Beat him!

Why did you steal?
He must be doing black marketing of vaccination.
I am not a thief. I am scared of needles. If the dose were less, I would have escaped. That's why, I stole two boxes. please forgive me.
Where are those two boxes?
In society's garbage bin.
Arjun gets the two boxes from the bin.
Now go to jail.
Uncle, please forgive him.
Ok

Well done kids!! Thank you !!
Uncle thanks to gabbar
Thank you, Gabbar!
Bhaiya, why are you not wearing a mask?
Now I am vaccinated.
The danger has not gone yet.
Ha ha! This time it's for 12- 18 years old children by Cadilla vaccination camp.
Another notice.
100%.
MY LIFE, MY VACCINE.

CHILDREN LITERATURE

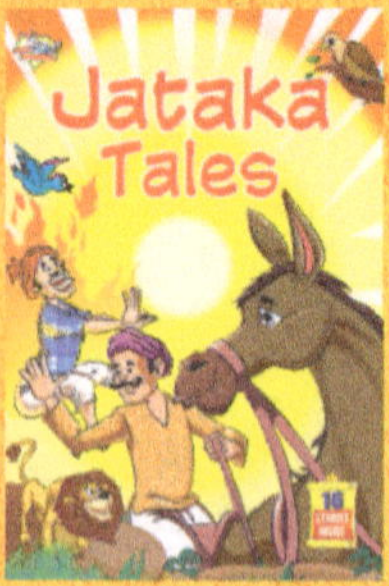

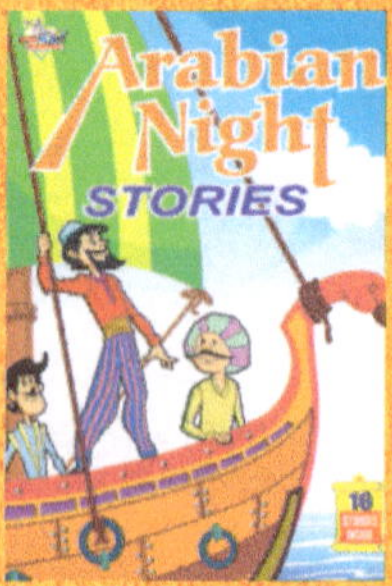

COLOURING & ACTIVITY BOOKS

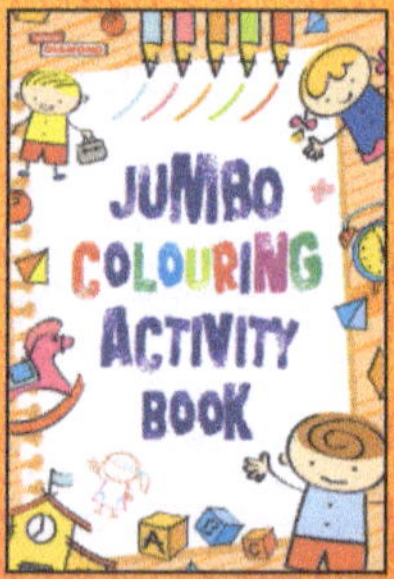